Waiting Rooms of the Heart

Waiting Rooms of the Heart

Poems of a Health Care Chaplain

Josie Gable Rodríguez

Blessings,
Josie Gable Rodriguez

iUniverse, Inc.
New York Lincoln Shanghai

Waiting Rooms of the Heart
Poems of a Health Care Chaplain

iUniverse books may be ordered through booksellers or by contacting:

iUniverse
2021 Pine Lake Road, Suite 100
Lincoln, NE 68512
www.iuniverse.com
1-800-Authors (1-800-288-4677)

Cover photograph by Sister Rebecca Rodríguez, CSJ
Saint Joseph of Orange Motherhouse, Orange County, California.

ISBN: 0-595-33972-7

Printed in the United States of America

Dedication

To my patients, their families, and my hospice and hospital colleagues—for lessons learned.

To my dad, Joseph George Gable, and brother, Peter Joseph Gable—for what their lives and the losing of them also taught me.

And to my husband, Al, and our sons, David, Gabriel and Benjamin—for their love and support through it all.

Contents

Appreciation

My heartfelt thank you to my family, friends and colleagues for your encouragement, support, and insight. And deep appreciation to all of my patients and their families who were the inspiration for my words.

To those who read my manuscript and offered suggestions. To Al, my husband of 39 years, Sister Rebecca Rodríguez, CSJ, for the cover photograph; Sue Diaz, dear friend and writer/author; First Sunday Writing Group; Nancy Ruppert, social worker and supervisor, San Diego Hospice; Mary Lee Buess, chaplain, Sharp Mary Birch Hospital; Charles Von Gunten, M.D., Ph.D., San Diego Hospice; Deborah Lindholm, director, Foundation for Women; Mary Curran-Downey, San Diego Union Tribune columnist; Fr. Bernie F. Cassidy, S.J.; Fr. Barry Martinson, S.J.; Karalee Davis, R.N., San Diego Hospice; John Fox, author, poet, teacher, friend.

How far you go in life depends
on your being
tender with the young,
compassionate with the aged,
sympathetic with the striving and
tolerant of the weak and strong.
Because someday in life you
will have been all of these.

—George Washington Carver

"Poetry puts words together in imaginative ways...and reveals what we don't know consciously but inherently recognize."

—John Fox, *Poetic Medicine: The Healing Art of Poem Making*

Introduction

As a clinical chaplain in hospital and hospice settings, I have experienced many instances of "waiting." Waiting for the right moment to enter a patient's room, waiting through silences and tears, waiting for family to arrive in the ER, for tough decisions to be made in the ICU, for the physician to break sad news or pronounce a death. In the Family Birth Unit I've waited for a new mother's labor to begin, or for the delivery of an infant who would be born too soon. Patients wait for meals, for someone to answer their call bell, for diagnostic tests, for the doctor to arrive, and for pain medication. Families, huddled together for support, wait in the hallways, the surgical waiting room or trauma center. Loved ones wait in the lobby, the chapel, at home by the phone. Home hospice patients wait for their nurse, chaplain, social worker, home health aide, or the interdisciplinary team to arrive to offer their expertise and loving care.

Shortly before my friend, Jackie died, after a long battle with cancer, she said, " I feel like I'm in a waiting room, a waiting place." Her words became the inspiration for the title of my book as I began to see that these experiences of waiting were all, waiting rooms of the heart.

Waiting wasn't something I felt I could do when it came to putting such life-changing experiences into words. In fact, I've been writing poetry for more than 30 years. When my three sons were very young I wanted to capture, like "word photographs," my experiences of being a mom; the tough and frightening times, and the moments of beauty and grace. Writing was a cathartic and tangible way for me to share with other moms our collective experience. Writing connected our truth and authenticity. And just as my sons brought poetry into my life, as together we learned the dance of family relationships, my patients and their families also brought poetry into my life.

Poetry, I've learned, encompasses different levels of awareness. In addition to the actual words meant to convey what each poem has to say, there are also those physical and emotional spaces between the lines of the poem, where the reader consciously or unconsciously adds their own experience and meaning.

I wrote these poems, *Waiting Rooms of the Heart*, as a tribute to the many patients and families I had been privileged to meet through my work. It was my way to remember them and to honor their strength and courage. I felt compelled to do this. As another writer, Lorna de Cervantes, once said, "I started writing for the same reason I breathe, because I had to." These poems took on lives of their own as they were written and revised over a period of seventeen years.

A CHAPLAIN'S ROLE

Chaplaincy for me began after many years of teaching adult education—a change of career from classroom to hospital. My one-year internship in Clinical Pastoral Education, theological graduate work and certification through the National Association of Catholic Chaplains gave me the education I needed to be a clinical chaplain.

Nurses and physicians take physical vital signs using stethoscopes, hands and assessment skills of listening to a person's heart and lungs, watching for signs of illness. This action is critical in determining the physical health of patients. What I learned in my training was to look for another vital sign, the vital sign of the spirit. It took a very special patient to make me aware of this. Catherine, age 38, had been a patient in our hospital for 20 days. She had come from another city to escape an abusive relationship. She had just moved into a shelter when she fell and severely broke her leg. Her job possibilities, shelter and dreams of a new life were shattered along with the bones in her leg. I saw Catherine almost daily during her stay and as the process of pastoral care continued, she told me of her past bouts with depression. I did what I could to help, offering daily prayer, healing touch, listening, and acceptance as part of my spiritual intervention. As I learned more about Catherine, I learned that she had a Masters degree in counseling and that she had done extensive research in her field. She told me one day, just before she was ready to be discharged from the hospital, "The nurses listened to my heart and lungs and took my pulse, all important, but you, Josie, you listened to the vital signs of my soul."

As chaplains we are observers and witnesses to pain, sorrow, anguish, courage, grief, acceptance and joy. But we are more than just passive observers. Just as physicians and nurses represent certain attributes and interventions, so too, does the chaplain. Our patients come from diverse cultural and religious traditions, and it is often the chaplain who helps bridge the vast distance between the medical and the spiritual. In day-to-day work, a chaplain may prepare a family in saying good-bye to a loved one in the emergency room, or begin the dialogue with a large family in the Intensive Care Unit on the importance of knowing patient wishes, or sit at the table of a hospital ethics committee, or officiate at a funeral or memorial service.

Here is what some chaplains have said about their work.

"The privilege of walking with others on their spiritual journey is one of the main reasons that I am a chaplain."

"As a chaplain, I hope that my ministry to each patient will help them realize God's compassion within themselves."

"Chaplaincy is more than a profession. It is a ministry, a calling to support the spiritual in oneself and others."

"I believe in the spiritual dimension of the person and that the spiritual needs healing as much as the physical or emotional."

Our professional role as chaplains takes us into the lives of patients and family members. We walk with them on their journey. We tell them by word and action that they will not be abandoned. We spiritually companion them like the Gaelic phrase, "anam cara," so beautifully describes as "soul friend."

Lawrence Holst, author of *Hospital Ministry, The Role of the Chaplain Today*, said, "The chaplain enters the struggle, hears the cries, listens to the story and joins the person in the pilgrimage of mystery and paradox." He continues, "When one enters the privacy of another's suffering, one is indeed on sacred ground."

That is what I believe good chaplains do—pay close attention to the spiritual suffering and distress of their patients and families.

Documentation, an important and necessary task, requires that we look at the problem, goal of care and the intervention, terms coming from a medical rather than spiritual model. I believe that we as chaplains need to be as comfortable with the language of medicine as we are with the language of spirituality and religion.

Spiritual care intervention takes on many forms—prayer, blessing, devotional rituals, active listening, facilitating discussions relating to the patient's meaning of life; the meaning of illness including cultural and religious beliefs; forgiveness, dialogue about dying and death. Supporting families and staff, providing resources and advocacy, encouragement, affirmation, and our presence are all an important part of care. The word "care" found in "pastoral care" comes from the Anglo-Saxon form, "kara", meaning to lament, to mourn, to cry out with, to participate in suffering.

As active participants in the suffering and joy of others I hope that we can follow what noted Theologian, Henri Nouwen, said during a presentation on the subject of compassion, "…to be the way, without being in the way." Listening, more than giving advice or suggestions; being more ecumenical than proselytizing; serving as a team member rather than acting alone—these are important dimensions of chaplaincy work.

In my work with adults as well as children I have often used complementary therapy interventions such as guided imagery, aromatherapy, music and art therapy. I remember one young patient telling me that she loved doing artwork. We gathered magazines, scissors and glue and during one of our visits she created a wonderful collage which she placed on her wall for all to see. She was very proud of that work as she explained the meanings behind the images, which included her hopes and dreams of completing high school.

She worked very hard to accomplish that goal and graduated with her class.

A VIEW FROM THE OTHER SIDE

I don't think that one can fully understand what it is like to be a family member of an acutely ill and dying loved one until you are that family member. Sitting in a small, crowded conference room with one window, trying to sleep, sharing hospital blankets and paper water cups was what I experienced one December evening with my family.

One day my father was playing golf, and two days later fighting for his life after a massive heart attack. He was brought to the same hospital where I worked as a chaplain. He died four days before Christmas. Eighteen months later, while at work as a pediatric hospice chaplain I received a phone call that my youngest brother was losing his battle with a rare form of cancer. I experienced what it was like to be on the other side of the fence, to be the family crying, questioning, advocating, grieving.

I have included in *Waiting Rooms of the Heart*, poems surrounding my brother's illness and death—for that profound experience affected my process as a chaplain with other patients and their families. These two experiences of the death of my father and brother changed my perception of what family members truly need and within those moments, pastoral care theory became pastoral care reality.

Throughout my years as a chaplain I was often struck by what I call the "on-goingness" of ordinary life within the hospital environment of trauma, illness and tragedy. As those things swirled around me, I couldn't help but also be aware of the loveliness life continued to offer. Employees enjoying a lunch hour in the sunshine, children giggling as birds splashed in the fountain near the hospital's main entrance, people in lobbies and elevators chatting about this and that, good weekends, or sporting events. And I was struck, too, by the sacredness of it all. Hurried staff members, beeping pagers, surgery schedules, I.V.'s, wheelchairs, cups of coffee, X-rays, waiting families, prayers, smiles, flowers, tears—the moments of life and death, moments of holding on and letting go, moments of grace.

"What sustained you as you did this type of work for so long? How did you care for yourself?" people often asked me. It was not always easy, but the loving support and affirmation from family and friends, quiet prayer and solitude, striving for balance between home and work, enjoying and celebrating life through nature, artwork and writing helped me. Paying attention to where I was spiritually was an important factor in helping to provide spiritual care to others.

Since that time long ago when I wrote poetry about my little boys digging in the garden and playing with snails, those boys have grown into fine young men of whom I am very proud. I read those poems written during that time in my life, and I remember. In this book, I read what I've written about those whose lives have touched mine in ways that even poetry can't completely express—Alma, Ruben, George, Marjorie, Susan, Peter and all the rest—and once again, I remember. Healing, self-discovery, personal growth, self care are the gifts we receive when we write our experiences as poem or journal entry. I invite you along.

"Heart, who will you cry out to?"
—Rainer Maria Rilke

We Remember Them

In the rising of the sun and in its going down,
we remember them.
In the blowing of the wind and in the chill of winter,
we remember them.
In the opening of buds and in the rebirth of spring,
we remember them.
In the warmth of the sun and the peace of summer,
we remember them.
In the rustling of the leaves and the beauty of autumn,
we remember them.
In the beginning of the year and when it ends,
we remember them.
When we are weary and in need of strength,
we remember them.
When we are lost and sick at heart,
we remember them.
When we have joys we yearn to share,
we remember them,
So long as we live, they too shall live,
for they are now a part of us,
as we remember them

—Jewish Remembrance

A Cup of Vanilla Bean Coffee

You fall, lying in the pain of broken bones at the base of a cliff far from here, in the dark, crying out for help, when no one listens, or comes for you until the sun rises over the hill.

In the haze of it all, you find yourself at a hospital where surgery is performed, where metal pins hold your bones together like glue. You wonder whether you need pins to hold your mind together.

You feel abandoned as you recover and ask, "Why don't the nurses believe my pain? No one is paying any attention to me. I am a person. I miss my son, I miss my son," she cries out. The tears fall—burning, guilt-ridden tears fall upon your hospital gown.

A prayer for healing, for direction, for focus, for your son, for you—two women trusting one another. We speak as two mothers, one in desperate need of special attention.

And, remembering that someone had recently brewed a fresh pot of coffee in the nurses' station; I offer you a cup. It's vanilla bean. The fragrance surrounds the air like sweet smelling, freshly baked cookies in a warm kitchen. Your hardened face softens as you accept this link between despair and hope, and turns to look at me with a delightful smile of feeling loved.

And She Dances

Like a wounded bird you sit propped
in a hospital bed in the middle
of your bedroom, beloved Siamese cat
at your side, the sound of oxygen
pumping, a long plastic lifeline
connected to the machine which helps you
breathe, thumping melodic sounds—
background music to the rhythms of
your heart.

You are angry and saddened by this disease
called ALS that robs you of your life and
your fifty years as a dancer.
Long-legged beauty shown in photos
on the wall, face the light, next to
grinning grandchildren.

You say that you are afraid of dying.
Afraid of the unknown.
So together we close our eyes and try
to imagine a place where you are whole,
where your limbs move at your command.

Where you take your mother's hand
and dance again.

Full Circle

The doctor came into the room
to explain to the family
that conditions had changed
for their mother.

That respirations were decreasing
and soon she would stop breathing
altogether.

The silent resignation.

The last good-bye of her daughter
who wondered,
What to do? What to say?

"No mother, not yet!"
"I'm not ready to let her go," she said.

But respirations became less and less.
The last breath, like the very first.

A slight sound.
The beginning of New Life.

Communion

Eucharistic body of Christ
through the body.
Body and people.
People of history and language.
The language of movement,
encountering,
growing,
moving toward a
liberating language of love.
Remembering.

Eucharistic body,
suffering servant.
Hope in and through
the Resurrection.
Movement toward metanoia,
a change of heart.

Eucharist believed
by the Hispanic family of fifteen
whose home was rebuilt
by college students.

Eucharist seen
in the eyes of a
young son
struggling to belong
but telling the truth instead.

Eucharist experienced
through the
rehabilitated heroin addict
touched by the expertise
of a dedicated doctor.

Eucharist observed
in the tearful eyes of an
elderly hospitalized patient
grateful for the attention
he had been given.

Eucharist understood
by the mother of her son
dying of A.I.D.S.

Eucharist meaningful beyond Jesus,
beyond the bread, beyond oneself.
Sacrament.

Bread broken, bread given.
Prophetic voice of justice
and service.

Flowers from Randy

Walking into his room he seemed
to recognize who I was, even though
I hadn't yet introduced myself.
"Can you come back this afternoon,
when I am less sleepy," he asked?

I looked at him.
And I waited,
fully expecting to come back at
another time.
He cried out, "I'm so afraid.
I don't want to die."
Tattoos covered his arms and neck
as skulls and demons slid across
skin and muscle wracked by pain.

"I don't want to hurt my mother, she's lost
one son already. She thinks I'm having tests.
I'm HIV positive. What am I going to tell
her? She'll be back Sunday."

He cried and cried.
"Forgive me for crying."
he said to me.
We speak of healing tears and wholeness.
He speaks of wanting a healed, peaceful heart.

He remembered long ago, when doing time in
State Prison, someone gave him a Bible.
He remembered a passage from scripture,
about a boat on the Sea of Galilee.
Randy remembered that everyone
on the boat was afraid,
afraid that the boat would sink.
Randy told me, "They are placing
all their trust and hope in the boat
and not in Jesus, who asked them not to be afraid.
I am that boat. I am sinking," said Randy,
"I don't know where to turn."

This man, his heart as big as the sun,
writes poetry and sends a single rose
to nurses who care for him.
As he begins to fall asleep, he says,
"Their smiles from ear to ear is all I need.
It's all I need."

I whisper to him and ask him to remember
the boat floating peacefully on the water.
"Jesus is smiling at you, Randy,
He is smiling at you from ear to ear."

I AM BEGINNING TO FORGET

For many years,
on the 18th and the twenty-first of each month,
I would remember my brother and my father
and the exact moment of their passing.
Time of day, place, who was present.

I remembered without
thinking—an automatic
response like breathing.

Both dates burned in the memory part
of my brain like strong magnets
holding photos of loved ones
to the front of a refrigerator door.

And it was a comfort.

Months and years have passed by, with many
Christmas celebrations and warm summer days.

I am beginning to forget, as the dates
go by without notice.

"Closure," some grief counselors would say.
But I have no closure for the sadness I feel
as I begin to forget.

I Want to Soar

Toward the end of a
warm summer day,
sunlight played
on the windowpane
near the chair where I sat.

Light reflected,
shadows flew,
moved,
danced.

I felt at that moment,
Marjorie's spirit begin to soar
toward Heaven.

Written two days before her death, Marjorie was one of my home care hospice patients. I asked her, on one of our visits, what she imagined her dying to be like and she said, "I want to soar." "Like the time you went soaring in a glider in Colorado? I asked, "Yes." said Marge.

Life Goes On

It seems strange to me that while
a young mother
miscarries her third baby;
and an infant in Special Care Nursery
struggles for life;
and a man jaundiced by liver cancer
reaches out for his wife's hand;
and a physician
grieves over the loss of his patient,
while worrying about his own family;
and a young boy
dies in the trauma room,
another victim of gang violence;
and a husband
prays for his beloved wife undergoing surgery;
and parents
sit with their gravely ill child;
while a mother in a darkened hospital room
whispers, "I love you"
to her son dying of A.I.D.S.;
it seems strange to me that
amidst these precious, individual lives,
and the crisis they face—
that life goes on.

It seems strange that young boys
in baggy pants
skateboard past the hospital with
energy and abandon;
while employees
sit in the sun by the fountain
enjoying their tuna sandwiches
brought from home.
People laugh,
lovers hug and hold hands.
The sun shines, heals and warms.
The springtime breezes pick up the
fragrance of a daffodil
and someone smiles.

Moment of Grace

A Vietnamese woman
sits next to an Indian
woman, who sits next to
an Anglo woman, who sits
next to an Ethiopian woman
in uncomfortable, sticky,
turquoise blue, vinyl chairs
facing the hallway, with
gurneys and wheelchairs
racing to the end,
like NASCAR drivers.

Languages are spoken in hushed
tones mixed together like the
fragrance of blended spices
in an open-air market.

Amidst all this activity I notice him,
an x-ray technician pushing a gurney
down the hall, looking more like
a football player than a hospital worker.

He gently lifts the frail elderly woman
from her wheelchair onto the starched
white sheet and covers her hurting body
with a toasty, warm blanket.

He carefully and slowly wheels her
to an X-ray room down the hall,
as her painful groans subside.
In this short moment of time
I witness a moment of grace.

Necessary Paperwork, Moments of Prayer

Documentation charts,
paper of every color,
interdisciplinary progress notes,
communication forms,
comprehensive plans of care, face sheets
with names like Suzanne, surrounded
by her many colorful pillows and Harry,
or Anna and Eileen with the big brown eyes;
dark-haired William, age three, and
Aaron, just fourteen, happy to have fully
reached his teenage years.

Yellow forms, pink, white and goldenrod
like streaks of sunlight.
Words stare at me in this pile of medical
facts, diagnosis, assessment, intervention,
plans and goals for future visits with patients
who struggle with hope for their future.

There will be no more plans or interventions
for patients whose names look at me from
stacks of documents, sorted through, one by one
and placed upon the darkened grill of my fireplace,
an altar celebrating tender memories, now
consumed by fire, becoming gray burning ash,
as I let them go.

First printed in *The Journal of Pastoral Care and Counseling*, Vol. 57, No.1, Spring, 2003

Matters of the Heart

Cardiac Unit
Heart patient #30527
Monitored heart.

Heart ache, heartbreak
Heart tests.
Stressed heart,
Heart-to-heart talk.
Years of pain, anger, work, hostility.
Straight from the heart.

Heart valve, heart strings.
Open heart.
Loss of Heart.

By-passed heart.
Grafted heart
Heartbeat.
Heart sounds
Relaxing mended heart.
Forgiving heart
Change of heart

As a chaplain for the Cardiac unit in an inner city hospital, I had the opportunity to observe the open-heart surgery of one of my patients.

Ode to my Pager

The small black pager assigned
to me from the hospice where I
work has codes typed on paper
in small letters attached to the side
for "urgent," "call now," "patient death,"
"co-worker waiting."

This pager sits in prominent display
on my night stand—like a pedestal,
turned on—alive—an
early warning system
of times to come during
these four nights of
"on call."

Airwaves magically
make the connection from
nurse to telephone
to the lighted display
on the top of this little
black box telling me whom to call
and how urgent the need.
Beep, beep, beep, beep—
a strange sound, I think,
for the notice of crisis, trauma or
death, and the grief which follows.
This call tells me that I must
go—soon.

I have the freeway all to myself
at two in the morning as I
drive the 20 miles to a hospital,
room number 24, where
seven adult children surround
their dying father.

Eyes turn together to look at me
as if one body, silently, expectantly
asking for comfort, for prayer,
for presence.

They draw me, like the gentle
surge of an ocean wave, into
their world of memory
through animated stories
told one by one, and
I know that this family
will heal from their grief
in the months and years ahead.

As I return home and crawl
back into bed to sleep, I place
my pager—this instrument of power
and communication on the night stand,
symbolically honoring all those
I've met on this cold winter
morning—and yet hoping that it's
power stays silent.

On Call

Today, the first day of January, my on-call rotation begins. I am the only chaplain "on" in the hospital, except for the on-call priest (call only for sacramental ministry).

I wonder, isn't my ministry sacramental as visit after visit in the trauma room, the intensive care unit, labor and delivery is made?

Ruben died this morning. A Jewish man mourned by his wife of sixty-two years. She cried from the depths of her heart as family members surrounded his hospital bed and listened to my prayers for them.

The young couple, whose pregnancy of thirty-two weeks ended too soon, a baby boy named Spencer died before birth, while sobs of his older brother carried throughout the Labor and Delivery unit, piercing the nurses' hearts.

A family's heartbreaking decision to remove a beloved elderly aunt from life-support in the Intensive Care Unit began this afternoon, and by evening, a code in the ER of a cherished father, 100 years-old, held by his daughter who said to him with the most compassionate and loving eyes, "Papa, it's all right. It's all right for you to go."

I went home late at night to a loving husband who made me chicken noodle soup with lots of garlic. And I lit a candle in honor of all who died today.

Peter's Hope

The doctor told him, "there is no hope."
Peter said that there was always hope.

Hope in the miracle of a new treatment.
Hope in leaving the hospital for home.
Hope in seeing his beloved wife, family
and friends.

Hope in petting his dog,
and picking vegetables from his garden
to eat on a warm summer day.

"Doctor, that is hope!"

Bright moonbeams came through
Peter's hospital window at night,
and sat on his bed during those
medicated moments of chemotherapy,
calling him home.

SEPTEMBER 11, 2001

Sinking into deep exhausted sleep
I woke at 3:00 A.M. 4:30 A.M. and then again at 8 A.M.
At each awakening I remembered—remembered
with a jolt—the images and events of two days before as two
airplanes, piloted by terrorists, sliced through top stories of
the World Trade Center—swift, surreal, angry blows to the
twin towers high above the streets of New York City.

Explosions enveloped these symbolic structures
of American wealth and power, filled with
office workers, mothers, fathers, brothers, sisters,
firemen, policemen, emergency medical teams,
children, tourists.
Windows and steel pillars
tumbled, tumbled and tumbled
inside out, outside in.

These twins died together, first one, then the other,
floor by floor, collapsed to the earth below creating thick,
billowing clouds of white smoke which appeared to chase
those still alive down the street like ghosts.

Smoldering ashes met the falling rain.
Tears from heaven, some said.
And our American flag, symbol of freedom and hope
rose amidst the honored grave site
of so many as our world took notice and wept.

As first published in *Vision Magazine*, September, 2002

To Shoulder a Burden

Shoulders

Have you ever thought
about them? We each have two.
We have one when the other
gives out on us.
Shoulders carry purses, backpacks,
babies, children, heavy jackets,
ill-fitted suits, skin, muscle, bone
and ligaments that sometimes snap
like rubber bands.
We massage our shoulders, shrug
and drop our shoulders.

Shoulders sometimes carry burdens.

Shoulders support arms and hands
that brace a bike, lift a load, mop the
floor, kayak a lake, stroke a face, arrange
a bouquet of flowers, remove obstacles,
pull weeds, knead bread, wave goodbye,
write a poem, wipe away tears, hug another,
greet, clasp and support with a touch.

Shoulders are the wings of birds
trying to fly. But what of the broken
wing, the wounded bird?

She sits and waits and dies a little.

Surgical Waiting Room

Fluorescent lights shine unnaturally
on top of silk ficus trees, plants made
to look real, separating groups
of brown leather chairs
facing each other,
where privacy is impossible.

Groups of families wait in the lobby
for news of loved ones in surgery
or the emergency room.
Magazines and newspapers read and reread,
bodies shifting forward, then back.
Arms extended overhead,
eyes staring straight ahead
or at the stale air, some heads bowed,
faces frozen in fear.

Tears, laughter, then tears
again and again and again.

Silence.

Good news, no news, bad news. Quiet
private conversations. Whispers of care
and compassion with long, loving hugs.

Sit, stand, no, sit again.

A military chaplain listens, watches and
holds a family, as news is brought,
like a bolt of lightening,
that their nineteen year-old son—new husband,
friend, brother, colleague—died after
three courageous days in the
Intensive Care Unit.
This family clings to one another as they walk
out of the hospital, into the bright sunshine,
while those of us who still wait,
grieve with them.

Observed and written while waiting with my mother for news of my sister coming out of surgery.

Ribbons of Memory

Ribbons of memory tie
like a package, interwoven
threads of faces and places
come to mind for me at the
most unexpected times of the
day or night.

For no apparent reason
except for the impact they had
on me when they were
my patients, when I would
visit them in their homes
and hospice rooms, where they
would share their acceptance
and peace—sometimes their
sadness and anger—in their dying.

As these threads of memory
surround me, tie me interwoven
like a package, I sometimes
wonder whether these patients
who have died, are trying to tell
me something, or maybe they
just want to be remembered.

SUSAN'S GUIDED MEDITATION

Susan's chiseled face, made thin by cancer
and its treatments, beautiful alabaster skin,
reminding me of a Greek goddess,
quiet and still.
But this living statue sits propped up in bed
surrounded by multi-colored pillows in her
bedroom by the sea, afraid to journey forward.

Unable to let go we take an imaginary trip together,
just she and I, to the ocean.
Lying on inflatable rubber mats in the
vast ocean, we let the sun warm our bodies,
while cool water tickles our toes, the
strong fragrance of white plumeria surrounds us.

Waves of water moved us to the edge of the shore
and back to the center and to the edge again.
And when it was time, Susan let go of my hand,
the gentle current taking her out to sea, while being
touched by the loving memory of her mother and sisters
surrounding her on this sunny, October day.

Tea Lady

Your collection of teapots and teacups
of varying sizes and styles sits in the antique
cupboard on glass shelves.

I remember our ritual of "tea and a muffin"
every time I visited with you at your home
on the hill overlooking the vast Pacific.

You can no longer serve tea, as you loved to do.
You can no longer dress yourself in your elegant
style or sit in your favorite chair by the corner
window, filtered bright light outlining your fragile
body, mentoring me about life and death.

I will miss you dearly, my lady.
And our time for tea.

Dedicated to Marjorie, age 84.

The Visit

From San Ysidro
to Oceanside
I drive along with traffic
so heavy that cars inch along
the freeway well below
the speed limit, and I must
remember to check the mileage
from one place to another.
I must remember to document
one patient and the other.
I must remember
to remember the
stories, and who I will visit
along the way.

When Heaven Welcomed Peter

When heaven welcomed Peter
the cool night air was as still and sweet
as a newborn baby sleeping.
And the night sky—
the milky way glistened
like diamonds falling—caught by
a crescent, macaroni moon.

When heaven welcomed Peter
the smell of sage and wet new-mown
grass filled the air, as thunderous
cascades of water
fell from North Lake
high in the Big Pine peaks.

After heaven welcomed Peter
the clouds high above the
Eastern Sierras edged with silver
formed magnificent, majestic swirls
over the mountains he loved so much.

And toward evening on the second day
the sun set radiantly, causing shades
of purples and blues to form above
the hot desert floor.

Peter's world of mountains and streams,
fish and frosty October mornings were
honored in that moment of pure beauty
as he looked at us from heaven.

Peter struggled for nine years with a cancer called, germ cell teratoma of the mediastinum, a tumor in his chest wall. He had many surgeries, days and nights of chemotherapy, and a stem cell transplant. He was one of the most courageous persons I have ever known. He and his wife, Joan, lived at the base of the Eastern Sierra Mountains near Bishop, California and enjoyed fishing, hiking, skiing and his job as a Park Ranger. He always had hope. He was my youngest brother and I miss him.

Words, Words and More Words

I visit you as I do each week, bringing
the ritual and comfort of Communion
and companionship during your journey of dying.
But today there is no comforting you.
You are angry—your words fly out like
bees around a nest. You say to me, "I'm sorry."
There is no need for apology from you as your brain
swells and causes you to say things you wouldn't ordinarily
say. But you know, and you can't control the stinging
words flowing from your mouth.

You want desperately to live. You have so many things
you still want to do—the treasures you once held and
dusted and placed gently on a shelf surround you—giving
protection. How can I possibly know what you are going
through? I've not walked your walk and yet must help
you in your walking.

You stand there naked and I in my
blue dress—you stare right through me.
I can't touch the depths of your sadness
and anger about this disease which will
kill you too young. How can I possibly know?
Words I say don't make much sense—to either of us.
I think it is I who should apologize.

SPIRITS IN THE WIND, SEPTEMBER 11, 2002

Wind swirled around the circle of honor as family members and friends mourned and remembered the 2,901 known dead during the memorial service in "the pit" at ground zero. Sacred ground in New York City.

Were these spirits in the wind?

"This grief is more than we can bear," the mayor said last year, when the winds came down and around, with choking dust and debris, wanting to swallow everyone in sight.

Today, as prayers were said and moments of silence honored, dust and flower petals rose up in tiny circles, touching tear-streaked faces and tousling the hair of grieving families standing on sacred ground.

A strong presence of those who died on that spot was felt in the clouds of dust as parents, children, wives, husbands, siblings, grandparents, friends and neighbors felt strangely comforted by precious spirits in the wind.

Twenty Nine Patients

Medical Surgical Unit/Morning Nursing Report

Liver Cancer, Multiple Myeloma, A.I.D.S,
Pneumonia, Breast Cancer, Stroke,
Altered Mental Status, Cancer of Esophagus,
Diabetes, Pleural Effusion, Wasting Syndrome,
Agranulocytosis, Metastatic Lung Cancer,

Spinal Tumor, Acute Leukemia, Gastroparesis,
Hepatic Encephalopathy, Urosepsis, Cellulitis,
Papillary Necrosis, Anemia, Bacerimia, Syncope
Defective J-Tube, Breast Cancer, Pneumonia,
Diabetes, Dehydration, Weakness, Stroke.

The list read like well-worn pages of a medical student's textbook. But these illnesses were attached to names like Nelly, Carmen, Samuel, Christopher, Isabel and Zacarais whose ages ranged from 24 years to 95. Some of these patients had been in the hospital for only a day, and one for 137 days—over four months of uncertainty—and the fogginess of medicated nights.

I am to be the bearer of hope, faith, acceptance and letting go. But how can I bring this presence to my patients today? Their pain and suffering momentarily fills me with consuming sadness and pulls me into their lives as the fast descent of the 7th floor elevator takes me to the hospital lobby where their friends and family members wait.

Prayer for Health Care Workers

Make me an instrument of your health.
Where there is sickness
let me bring care;
Where there is injury, aid.
Where there is suffering, ease.
Where there is sadness, comfort.
Where there is despair, hope.
And where there is death,
acceptance and peace.
Grant that I may not seek so much
to be consoled, as to console.
To be understood, as to understand.
To be honored, as to honor.
It is in giving of ourselves that we
heal and it is in listening
that we comfort.

Adapted from the Prayer of Saint Francis

I was hungry,
and you gave
me food.

I was thirsty
and you gave
me drink.

I was lonely
and you made
me welcome.

I was naked
and you
clothed me.

I was ill
and you
came and
looked after
me.

I was in prison
and you came
to see me there.

For whatsoever you
do to others,
even the least,
You do to me.

—Matthew 25:35–36

The Children

"A butterfly lights beside us like a sunbeam, and for a brief moment its glory and beauty belong to our world. But then it flies on again. And though we wish it could have stayed, we feel lucky to have seen it." This beautiful image, author unknown, signifies for me, the experience of caring for children with life-threatening and life-limiting illnesses.

Many of the infants and children I encountered through my work were with their parents for such a short time. The sadness, which followed their loss, was palpable, as was the tremendous love their parents had for them. The caring and support for these children from family and staff were always moments of grace for me.

How often have we heard the comment, "the loss of a spouse or parent is terrible, the loss of a child, devastating." For the first eleven years as a chaplain I worked within an acute care inner-city hospital in Pediatrics, Labor and Delivery, Special Care Nursery and Family Birth Center. Spiritual care was an important area of support when families experienced pre-term labor, pregnancy loss, life-threatening illness of their infant, and neonatal death. I was called to Labor and Delivery one morning. Staff alerted me to a 15 year-old girl, four months pregnant. Her baby had no fetal heart tones. She was told this as her body began the long process of labor. This young girl asked those of us in her room, "When my baby is born will he cry?" The doctor and nurses had tears in their eyes as they gave their answer.

My experience as Pediatric Chaplain in hospice gave me added perspective as to what parents need and want during their child's illness and death and what children need when a parent, grandparent or sibling dies. As a home health chaplain, I, along with the interdisciplinary team, visited patients and their families, from infants to late teens, in their homes. Hospice is about hope and living. It is offering choices about quality of life and healing and creating cherished memories through activities like making handprints and memory boxes. I provided opportunities for prayer and blessing, sacraments, supportive active listening, offering resources, assisting with plans for the funeral or memorial service and being present. My desire was to help parents know that they would not be abandoned through their child's illness and death. The courage and strength from these children and their parents were blessings to me.

An area close to my heart was the Early Intervention Program, a unique and very special service at San Diego Hospice, which provided compassionate care for families who had been told that their unborn baby had a life-threatening, life-limiting prognosis. From the moment of diagnosis, this program offered support from the chaplain, nurse, home health aid, social worker, and bereavement counselors according to the needs of the family.

Like the beautiful butterfly that stays only for awhile then flies on again, these children stayed for awhile, and affected us profoundly as their memory nestled within our hearts.

A Butterfly

A butterfly lights
beside us
Like a sunbeam.
And for a brief
moment
Its glory and beauty
Belong to our world.

But then it flies on again.

And though we wish
it could have stayed
We feel lucky to
have seen it.

Author Unknown

A Mother's Prayer

Dear God, Bless this child in my womb
this life, which is so wanted and precious
to us. The baby's movements remind me
that all is well, but labor has begun too soon.
With every premature contraction
there is the fear that our baby will be
born too early.
I try to relax, but sometimes they keep on coming.
I watch the heart rate on the monitor and hear
the beautiful heart beat. I ask you, God,
to quiet the contractions in my body,
to keep our baby safe and to give me
strength, to go through this time
of waiting with hope and acceptance.
Amen

Prayer for Parents Whose Baby has Died

May peace be with you
at this most difficult time,
the loss of your baby.
My prayer is that you,
mother and father,
grandparents,
brothers and sisters
feel the surrounding love and
comfort of God through your
family, friends and hospital staff.

It is so difficult to understand
and accept this terrible loss
and I ask that you be given
strength and courage during this time
and the days ahead.

This prayer can be adapted accordingly

ELVA

Hoped-for dreams, cut short by slowed heartbeats and then, no heartbeat at all.
"This is impossible. It can't be so. My baby was fine and now you say he is not?"
Labor room, small, cramped, filled with loving, questioning family members trying to comfort.

There are no words that can take away the pain as the I.V. drip begins the contractions which starts their child on its journey, a difficult passage into a world he will never know, and delivered into the arms of a young mother who asks, why?

They ask for a prayer and blessing as I move around the delivery room, nurses respectfully quiet as I pray.

"In the name of the Christian community I sign Andre with the sign of the cross and I invite his parents and those here present to do the same. God bless and be with Andre who felt the wonderful love of his parents, and I ask that God keep him in his loving care. Comfort Elva and John now and in the days ahead with the knowledge that You will always hold them close to Your heart."

John peers into the tiny face of his newborn baby. Tenderly touching his baby's body, he turns to look at his wife on the delivery table—feelings of shock and helplessness overwhelm him and he sobs openly.

Days spent in the hospital recovering, Elva holds her baby again and begins to think about a memorial service, and how her baby looks so perfect.

"Will I ever recover from this," she asks?
"I'm afraid to go home."

She sits carefully in a wheelchair and courageously prepares to leave the hospital, cradling in her lap a dozen red roses, remembering the dear life she once held.

Inspired by, and dedicated to the Labor and Delivery nurses and the Family Birth Unit at Scripps Mercy Hospital, San Diego, California.

Baby William

A rose I picked for you today,
the petals peachy pink, like newborn skin.
(I wanted you to have something to hold).

To smell the sweet fragrance and feel
the softness surround your hurting heart.
You held this long-stemmed beauty throughout
your son's memorial service.
(I wanted you to have something to hold).

Words of comfort, sobs of sorrow as light
rain fell on the rose and toys you so
tenderly placed in the grave of your
toddler son who died too soon.

And like the flight of a hummingbird,
bright yellow balloons rose to meet
tears falling from the sky.
(I just wanted you to have something to hold).

This little boy was my first pediatric hospice patient—a young family that touched my heart.

Empty Aching Arms

Empty, aching arms surround
your heart, like loosely tied ribbons
in a child's hair ready to drop to
the ground.

Empty, aching arms throb
with the memory of a hoped-for
child, but lost in an instant,
like the soft sounds of
chimes blowing softly
in the distant breeze.

How does one accept that your unborn child has a life-threatening or life-limiting disease? As a chaplain for the Pediatric Early Intervention Team I was assigned to a young couple. As I left their home after my first visit I noticed that my arms were aching, as if I had held something very heavy. The ache didn't go away for a few hours. It was then that I realized that what I felt was the loss that this young woman would soon endure, and the memory of my own loss through four miscarriages twenty-five years earlier.

Michael Who Was Three

Michael woke this cloudy
March morning to tell his
mama and papa,
"Don't cry, I love you."
He then slipped into a
sacred place surrounded
by tearful, loving parents
and attentive, compassionate
hospice staff, who touched
and caressed his little body
as his tender young spirit
soared into the arms of God.

Mother and Child

I watch as your 18-month old baby daughter climbs up on the chair carefully placed next to your hospital bed, a bed covered with papers, books, bills and receipts, and she snuggles.
She moves her little head next to yours on the pillow.
A moment of time I am privileged to see.

Your little one only knows something is different.
That you are spending more days in bed.
That you can't pick her up like you did before because of the pain in your side.
The cancer spreading like wildfire in your belly.

This tousled, brown-haired beauty climbs down, curls up on the floor holding her warm blanket and falls asleep, dreaming of her mother's love.

"Oh, she is asleep," you say.
And your face takes on the glow and peacefulness of contentment as you whisper,
"She will remember me, I know she will."

Another courageous patient who did everything she could to make life better for her children after her death. Together we made handprints of this mother and child and printed them on a bright purple memory box for her young daughter to have when she was older—to help her remember.

Mother Job

The pain of losing her little boy of seven years was too much to bear.

Her tightly clenched fist raised up to the sky as if to punch the floor of heaven to ask God, "Why?"

"I am Job," she said, "I feel like how he must have felt—the man in the Bible who so long ago asked the same question."

Rose Petals for Angelica

Time has come, the family gathered together to say goodbye to their much loved seven year old daughter, grand daughter, niece, cousin, friend who wanted to sing like Selena.

Time has come, the family gathered together to watch, to bear witness to her little spirit move from this world to the next, her peaceful face showing no pain or distress.

Time has come, the family gathered together to pray, to bless with rose oil Angelica's forehead as I have done—each member of her family, cousins and little friends taking turns—quietly, respectfully, cautiously.

Time has come, the family has gathered together to wait. They know the time is near.

A very quiet moment and she is gone.

No wailing or outbursts of anger, but quiet tears and acceptance as Angelica's little friends and cousins pick rose petals from her grandfather's garden and sprinkle them around her body, as if to protect Angelica from any more pain.

Early Morning Reflection

Two families struck by the tragedy of man.

A teenaged boy traveling too fast down a busy street.
A family outing and in an instant, screaming brakes,
lives changed forever.

Agony.

Do you know what agony looks like?

I saw it on the faces of the young fathers who lost their children, one twelve years old, ready for the excitement of Jr. High School and the other little girl, just three, full of life and laughter only a toddler can bring.

Their mothers—faces close together in an understanding embrace of grief—say to each other,
"At least they died together."
These parents move in slow motion around the small family conference room.
"Are you sure?" "It has to be a mistake."
"Tell me it isn't true."

Our hospital is eerily quiet, as if in reverence for these young lives lost. And as the darkness of early morning breaks into daylight, disbelief becomes heart-wrenching reality as the work of grief begins.

Ways This Book Can Be Used

In his book, *Poetic Medicine: The Healing Art of Poem-Making*, John Fox says, "Poetry is a natural medicine, it is like homeopathic tincture derived from the stuff of life itself—your experience. The exciting part of this process is that poetry used in this healing way helps people integrate the disparate, even fragmented parts of their life. Poetic essences of sound, metaphor, image, feeling and rhythm act as remedies that can elegantly strengthen our whole system—physical, mental and spiritual. The moment of surprising yourself with your own words...is at the heart of poetry as healer."

John Fox says so beautifully what I have been feeling throughout the years of writing these poems. It occurred to me that other chaplains and those in care giving professions might benefit from writing down their experiences in poetic form as well. I had been inspired by the work of the Association for Poetry Therapy. Physicians and nurses were writing poetry, why not chaplains?

Presenting the class, "Writing Poetry As A Means Toward Self Care" to Clinical Pastoral Education interns and residents at Sharp Memorial Hospital in San Diego, California, was not only a successful project but a thrilling experience for me to see their process as hospital chaplains and to hear the resulting poetry. It was wonderful. I know that a few have continued with their writing.

I have recently begun poetry sessions with women who have life-threatening illnesses who meet monthly for support through the San Diego Foundation for Women.

I envision *Waiting Rooms of the Heart* being used with

- Medical school interns and residents
- Student nurses
- Clinical Pastoral Education interns
- Theology students
- Graduate programs in nursing
- Graduate programs in pastoral counseling
- Life-threatening illness support groups

Used with some facilitation, these poems could be starting points for writing poetry about personal experiences where the discussions surrounding the poetry could be honest and insightful, and as John Fox has said, "…a voice that says that you are not alone."

Helpful Resources

Association for Clinical Pastoral Education
1549 Clairmont Road, Suite 103
Decatur, GA 30033-4611

Association of Professional Chaplains
1701 East Woodfield Road, Suite 311
Schaumburg, IL 60173

National Association of Catholic Chaplains
3501 South Lake Drive
P.O. Box 070473
Milwaukee, WI 53207-0473

National Association of Jewish Chaplains
901 Route 10
Whippany, NJ 07981

San Diego Hospice
Pediatric and Early Intervention Program
4311 Third Avenue
San Diego, CA 92103-1407

The National Association for Poetry Therapy
16861 SW 6th Street
Pembroke Pines, FL 33027

Recommended Books

Nine Gates: Entering the Mind of Poetry, Jane Hirshfield

Poetic Medicine: The Healing Art of Poem-Making, John Fox

Sutured Words: Contemporary Poetry about Medicine,
Jon Mukand, Editor

The Healing Heart, Rafael Campo

The Heart Aroused: Poetry and the Preservation of the Soul in Corporate America, David Whyte

To Be the Poet, Maxine Hong Kingston

About the Author

Josie Gable Rodriguez attended San Diego State University with a Bachelor of Arts degree in Speech Pathology. She received her Master of Arts in Practical Theology from the University of San Diego. She completed four units of Clinical Pastoral Education at Sharp Memorial Hospital, San Diego, with certification since 1987 through the National Association of Catholic Chaplains. She holds membership in the National Association for Poetry Therapy, and the National Red Cross Spiritual Response Team.

Josie has published articles in *Healing Ministry, Health Progress, Journal of Critical Care Nursing, Journal of Pastoral Care and Vision*, a National Association of Catholic Chaplains publication. She has been a presenter both locally and nationally in the area of spiritual care within a health care setting.

She and her husband live in San Diego where they open their home for classes in art, book arts, journal and poetry writing. Josie can be contacted at www.yagottahaveart.com.

web page
josierodriguez.com

e-mail
josierod1@cox.net

0-595-33972-7

Printed in the United States
47507LVS00002B/1-153